- Let the fire of God destroy all those in possession of my delayed and detained Blessings. They shall be roasted without recognition in Jesus Name Amen

- By the authority of the word of God, I break every curse of delayed blessings operating in my life in Jesus name.

- I break every curse of delayed blessings operating in the life of our fore fathers that have been transferred to my life into ~~peaces~~ PIECES in Jesus Name Amen.

- I received strength from God the Father to break through the troops of the enemy to recover all without losing anything in the name of Jesus.

- Let the angels of the living God roll away every stone of hindrance to the manifestation of my breakthroughs in the name of Jesus.

- I command every wall of Jericho standing between me and my destiny to collapse, and never to rise again in Jesus mighty name

- I m redeemed from all curses ancestral, paternal, martially and from every form of delay and detained blessing in the name of Jesus.

- I bind, plunder and cast out of my life, every anti-breakthrough, anti-blessings and anti-testimony spirits in the name of Jesus

- I command the release of my confiscated blessings in Jesus Name

- I command the powers that have swallowed my blessings to vomit them by fire in the name of Jesus.

Father God, order Hot Thunderbolt from Your Throne Room to Pass Through The Camp of The Enemy And I command The Release of all my delayed blessing, detained Blessing & confiscated Blessings Now in The Name of Jesus.

- I vomit all foods that I have eaten in my dreams and that is affecting my moving forward in Jesus Name Amen

- I break my known or unknown curses and covenants the enemy is holding onto, in order to withhold my blessings. Specifically mention any blessing in your live by name and command their release in the mighty name of Jesus.

- My success is precious to God. Let my blessing (delayed or detained) become like the ark of God to the Philistines, trouble the camp of the enemy with plague in Jesus Name.

- I receive divine assistance to recover all through the blood of Jesus. in The Name of Jesus

- I receive divine assistance to destroy the powers of all my enemies in Jesus Name.

- I refuse to continue to tarry in any satanic bus-stop; I must enter my destiny this year in the name of Jesus — God ordained destiny / Divine destiny

- Lord, let all evil labels fashioned by the camp of the enemy against my life be completely rubbed off now, in Jesus name. → with The Blood of Jesus

- With The Fire of God — I break myself loose from the bondage of stagnancy and delayed blessings in the name of Jesus Christ

- Holy Ghost fire destroys anything that makes your promises to fail or tarry in my life in Jesus name.

- I decree by the anointing of the Holy Spirit, the rapid fulfillment of all prophecies and promises of God concerning me in Jesus name

- Lord Jesus, let the angelic (rapid respond saquad) invade the camp of my enemy and recover all my long awaited blessings in Jesus name

- Having waited long for my breakthrough, I shall not be frustrated nor be disappointed in the end, in Jesus name

- Today, I activate the Abrahamic and the Messianic covenants operating in my life. By these divine covenants, let all my delayed blessings be released now in the name of Jesus. 8/12/16

- In Jesus mighty name I move from the back to the front of the queue of blessings in Jesus name

- Father, from hence forth, let my life be a divine magnet that attracts diverse miracles all the time. in The Name of Jesus

- I resist, bind and overthrow all miracle hijackers, miracle deflectors and miracle interceptors operating in and around me in Jesus mighty name.

- I shall fulfill prophetic words over my life and ministry in Jesus name.

1/2/17 Thurs
8/11/16 Thur

Day Two

Before you pray please follow the instructions below.

a. **Read the Bible Passage below** *Gate of Heaven .15 17*

   Genesis 28:1-4; 11-19; 31:38-42

b. **Confess all your sins, both known and unknown**

30 Prayer Points

> Every visible and invisible power delaying my manifestation this year, be destroyed in Jesus name

> Every Marine Powers delaying my blessings be roasted by fire in Jesus Name

- ➤ Book of generational failure, bearing my name, catch fire, in the name of Jesus. *(Roast to Ashes Now)*

- ➤ Every satanic court, summoned to deliberate on my progress, scatter, in the name of Jesus
  - ↳ by fire

- ➤ Father, break every covenant of delay operating in my life in Jesus name.

- ➤ Thou agent of darkness assigned to delay my due promotion and celebration, be arrested in Jesus name.
  - ↳ And chained with HOT FETTERS

- ➤ By divine authority, every virtue and goodness of my life delayed anywhere, come out by force in Jesus name.

- ➤ I silence every voice of darkness speaking negatively against my progress in Jesus name.

- ➤ **I receive the power of God to MOVE FORWARD, in every area of my life, in the mighty name of Jesus Christ.**

- ➤ I shall not die, but live to fulfill my God-given destiny, in Jesus' name.

- ➤ I command seven-fold restoration of everything the enemy has taken from me, in Jesus' name. *(+ my family)*

- ➤ **Fire of God, consume the evil clock of the enemy that is working against my life, in the name of Jesus.**

- ➤ **Oh LORD, restore my wasted years in Jesus' name.**

- ➤ **LORD, restore my wasted efforts, money, health, strength and blessings, in Jesus' name.**

- I remove from my life by fire every barrier to my breakthroughs in Jesus' name.

- I uproot and destroy from my life by the Holy Ghost fire every obstacle to my miracle, in Jesus' name.

- I break in pieces every horn scattering my blessings, in the name of Jesus Christ.

- I destroy every hedge the enemy has put over my blessings to prevent me from receiving them in my lifetime, in Jesus' name.

- Every evil power holding back my prayers, or the answers to my prayer, I command you to be bound, in Jesus' name. — *Hot fetters / Hot chains*

- I command all doors of good things, closed against me by the enemy to be opened, in the name of Jesus. *(Battering Ram)* — *immediately*

- I release my helper to come to me now, in Jesus' name.

- Every shadow of darkness the enemy has cast over me, to prevent my prosperity, job, business contacts, promotion, or breakthrough from locating me, I remove it by fire, in the name of Jesus Christ. *(prevent the sale of my house)*

- Let all hidden potentials and gifts that will make me great, stolen from me, be restored 21 fold, in the name of Jesus.

- I decree total destruction upon every personality that has vowed never to release to me anything God has destined for me, in Jesus' name.

- I break in pieces every covenant or curse obstructing divine restoration in my life, in Jesus' name.

Evil Trees dry up Now in The Name of Jesus
You will never ever produce Fruit Again

- Trees of problems in my life, dry up to the roots, in Jesus' name.
- Walls of physical and spiritual opposition, fall after the order of Jericho, in the name of Jesus
- Lord, make my case *(nephews)* a miracle. Shock my foes, friends, and even myself, in the name of Jesus.
- With the blood of Jesus Christ, I shatter every covenant that gives the enemy upper hand to take from me the blessings God has given to me, in the name of Jesus Christ.
- Lord, make my case a miracle. Shock my foes, friends, and even myself, in the name of Jesus. *Repeat*
- With the blood of Jesus Christ, I shatter every covenant that gives the enemy upper hand to take from me the blessings God has given to me, in the name of Jesus Christ.
- Every household wickedness eating up the blessings God Almighty has bestowed upon my life and family, I destroy you, in Jesus' name.
- I command a hundred-fold restoration of everything the enemy took from me when I was weak, in Jesus' name.

8/12/16 Fri

Day Three

Before you pray please follow the instructions below.

a. **Read the Bible Passage below**

   Isaiah. 6:1-8

a. **Confess all your sins, both known and unknown**

30 Prayer Points

- All acquired Spirit of delayed and detained blessings in my body be roasted by fire in Jesus Name Amen
- I reject every spirit of delayed and detained blessings planted in my mother's womb before I was born in Jesus Name Amen.
- Every power slowing down my progress in life, fail in Jesus name.
- Oh Lord, release divine empowerment for speed upon me today to overtake in every area of my delay in Jesus name
- Everything in and around me that is cooperating with the force of delay to delay me, scatter in Jesus name
- From today, I refuse to be delayed from progressing in Jesus name.
- My father and my God, call forth my delayed glory to shine from today in Jesus name.
- Every arrow of evil delay, fired into my star, die, in the name of Jesus.
- Every arrow of backwardness, fired into my star, die, in the name of Jesus.
- Chains of stagnation, break, in the name of Jesus

- Delay tactics, organized against my joy, scatter, in the name of Jesus.
- Every delay, programmed to tie me down, die, in the name of Jesus.
- Every arrow of disappointment, die, in the name of Jesus.
- Thou power of hard-life, die, in the name of Jesus.
- Every arrow of shame, targeted at my life, backfire, in the name of Jesus.
- Every power ordained to make me rise and fall, die, in the name of Jesus.
- Every power of my father's house, delaying my breakthroughs, die, in the name of Jesus.
- Curses and covenants of satanic delay, die, in the name of Jesus.
- Deep pit, swallowing my virtues, vomit them by fire, in the name of Jesus.
- Chain of delay, holding my star, break, in the name of Jesus.
- Cloud of darkness around my breakthroughs, scatter, in the name of Jesus.
- I pull down every stronghold of satanic delay, in the name of Jesus.
- Every strongman assigned against my progress, die, in the name of Jesus.
- Satanic decree over my picture, die, in the name of Jesus.

- Every evil power draining my virtues, die, in the name of Jesus.
- Failure and calamity shall not be my identity, in the name of Jesus.
- Power of stagnation, dry up, in the name of Jesus.
- Every padlock holding down my progress, catch fire, in the name of Jesus.

Day Four 8/13/16 Sat / Sat Nov 4, 2017

Before you pray please follow the instructions below.

a. **Read the Bible Passage below**

Psalm 105:17-22

a. **Confess all your sins, both known and unknown**

30 Prayer Points

- My wasted years, be restored by fire, in the name of Jesus.
- Every child of darkness, covering my future, catch fire, in the name of Jesus.
- Wind of the spirit, carry me to my destination, in the name of Jesus.
- I decree failure is not my portion, in the name of Jesus.

- Household strongman, assigned against my destiny, die, in the name of Jesus.
- Every anti-favor oil on my head, dry up, in the name of Jesus.
- Blessings from unexpected quarters, locate me by fire, in the name of Jesus.
- Covenant of hard labor of my father's house, die, in the name of Jesus.
- Holy Ghost fire, convert my delay to speed by fire, in the name of Jesus.
- Glory of the later house, catch up with my star, in the name of Jesus.
- O thou that troubleth the Israel of Mountain of Fire and Miracles Ministries, the God of Elijah shall trouble you today.
- Every enemy of the Mountain of Fire and Miracles Ministries, scatter, in Jesus' name.
- O God arise and uproot anything You did not plant inside the Mountain of Fire and Miracles Ministries.
- Let the fire of revival fall upon Mountain of Fire and Miracles Ministries, in the name of Jesus.
- **I remove the hand of household wickedness from my marital life, in the name of Jesus.**
- **Let every incantation, incision, hexes and other spiritually harmful activities working against me, be completely neutralized, in the name of Jesus.**

↳ by The Blood of Jesus

- I command all forces of evil manipulating, delaying or hindering my marriage *(The Sale of my house)* to be completely paralysed, in the name of Jesus
- Let all evil anti-marriage marks be removed, in the name of Jesus *from me with The Blood of Jesus*
- Lord, restore me to the perfect way in which you created me if i *or my D.N.* have been altered *in any way whatsoever.*
- Father, let your fire destroy every satanic weapon fashioned against my marriage, in the name of Jesus.
- Lord, expose all the schemes and plans of satan *which he* ever devise against me through any source and any time. *in The Name of Jesus*
- I forsake any personal sin that has given ground to the enemy, in the name of Jesus
- I reclaim all the ground I have lost to the enemy, in the name of Jesus' name.
- I apply the power in the name and blood of Jesus to my marital situation. *in The Name of Jesus*
- Thank God for His goodness and for all He has done for you this year.
- Father empower me to continue and prevail in prayer in Jesus' name.
- Lord, rekindle Your precious, holy and purifying fire in me, in Jesus' name.
- Spirit of God, draw me into a new and intimate relationship with You from now, in Jesus' name.

- ➢ Oh God, revive me, in every area of my life, in the name of Jesus Christ.

- ➢ Father God, teach me how to reach Your heart daily, and receive from You all the blessings you have in store for me, in Jesus' name.   ] *This*

(*) Activate Every Spiritual Blessing You have given me according to Ephesians 1:3

Day Five Sun 8/14/16
Sun 11/5/17

Before you pray please follow the instructions below.

a. **Read the Bible Passage below**

Psalm 105:17-22

a. Confess all your sins, both known and unknown

30 Prayer Points

- By the power of the Holy Spirit, I deliver myself from every financial bondage, in Jesus' name.

- I set myself free from bondage to failure, sickness, poverty, untimely death, retrogression, lack and failure at the edge of success, in Jesus name.

- Every power tying me down to one spot, PERISH! In the name of Jesus Christ.

- Every curse pronounced against my destiny, BREAK, in the name of Jesus Christ.

- Every curse militating against my prosperity, and the fulfillment of my goals, BE DESTROYED! In the name of Jesus.

- Every barriers of limitation assigned against me, SCATTER! In Jesus' name.

- Every objects fashioned against my life and family, be frustrated and disappointed, in the name of Jesus Christ.

- Any power assigned with the mandate to hinder and curse my prosperity, DIE! In Jesus' name.

- I destroy from my life every cycle of failure, disappointments, sickness and frustration, in Jesus' name.

- Every curse operating in my family line, BREAK! In the name of Jesus Christ.

- The forces of darkness assigned to tie me to one spot, I command you to PERISH! In the name of Jesus Christ.

- Father God, turn every curse I brought upon myself to blessings, in Jesus' name.

- Every mountain on my way to success and victory, be removed! In Jesus' name.

- I destroy by fire, every boundary the enemy has marked down for me, in Jesus' name.

- I break self-imposed stagnancy and limitations, in the name of Jesus Christ.

- I receive double portion blessings in exchange for my shame and delay, in Jesus' name.

- Thank God for answers to your prayers.

- Every curse that I have brought into my life through disobedience and ignorance, break by fire, in the name of Jesus Christ.

- Every unspoken curse against my life, family and business, break, in the name of Jesus Christ.

- Every curse militating against my prosperity, and the fulfillment of my goals, BE DESTROYED! In the name of Jesus.

- Every barriers of limitation assigned against me, SCATTER! In Jesus' name.

- Every objects fashioned against my life and family, be frustrated and disappointed, in the name of Jesus Christ.

- Any power assigned with the mandate to hinder and curse my prosperity, DIE! In Jesus' name.

- I destroy from my life every cycle of failure, disappointments, sickness and frustration, in Jesus' name.

- Every curse operating in my family line, BREAK! In the name of Jesus Christ.

- The forces of darkness assigned to tie me to one spot, I command you to PERISH! In the name of Jesus Christ.

- Father God, turn every curse I brought upon myself to blessings, in Jesus' name.

- Every mountain on my way to success and victory, be removed! In Jesus' name.

- I destroy by fire, every boundary the enemy has marked down for me, in Jesus' name.

- I break self-imposed stagnancy and limitations, in the name of Jesus Christ.

Day Six *Tues 10/6/20*
Mon 8/15/16

Before you pray please follow the instructions below.

a. **Read the Bible Passage below**

   I Corinthians. 15:8-10

a. **Confess all your sins, both known and unknown**

30 Prayer Points

- I receive double portion blessings in exchange for my shame and delay, in Jesus' name.

- Thank God for answers to your prayers.

- Every curse that I have brought into my life through disobedience and ignorance, break by fire, in the name of Jesus Christ.

- I destroy by fire all the horns assigned to scatter my prosperity, family, business and possessions, in Jesus' name.

- I demolish every stumbling block on my way to success, promotion and victory, in Jesus' name.
- Every good thing God has destined for me, but is in the possession of someone else, I command it to come to me now, in Jesus' name.
- I posses the power to pursue, overtake and recover my goods from spiritual Egyptians, in the name of Jesus.
- Let every spell, jinxes, and demonic incantations rendered against me be cancelled, in the name of Jesus.
- Lord, heal all wounds and spiritual bullets sustained from attacks of the enemy.
- Father, I pray, remove any person or personality sitting on my blessings, miracles, breakthrough, prosperity, finance, job or good health, in the name of Jesus Christ.
- All my possessions in the north, south, east or west, I command them to come to me now, in Jesus' name.
- All my possessions in the spirit realm, I release them into the physical by fire, in the name of Jesus Christ.
- I receive a hundred-fold restoration of all I have lost, in Jesus' name.
- I receive a hundred-fold restoration of everything the enemy stole from me, in the name of Jesus Christ.
- Lord, give me power for a new beginning. in The name of Jesus
- Thank God for answers to your prayers.

- Generally, favour means goodwill, acceptance and the benefits flowing from these.
- It is also used interchangeably with mercy, grace and kindness.
- Favour is that which helps man to achieve divine destiny or expectation with minimum effort.
- Favor adds flavor to our lives and mobilizes others to help us in accomplishing our destiny plans and dreams.
- When the spirit of favour is upon our lives, it compels men and spirits to assist us in our destiny pursuits.
- Favor spares us the ordeals of unnecessary or needless labour and toiling.
- Favor makes our countenance or presence appealing and endearing to prospective helpers.
- The spirit of disfavor, on the other hand, makes our presence repulsive to those who ought to help us.

> Favor is that which moves others to help and encourage you.

> Without favour, destiny fulfillment will suffer needless delay or abortion.

> Father, forgive my sins and give me grace to live a life that attracts your favour.

> By the blood of Jesus, I receive cleansing from every deposit of rejection through sin.

> In the name of Jesus, I break the power of evil magnetism and negative aura.

Day Seven ~~(SKIP)~~

Before you pray please follow the instructions below.

a. **Read the Bible Passage below**

   Isaiah 60:1

a. **Confess all your sins, both known and unknown**

   IF YOU ARE BARREN YOU NEED TO PRAY TO GET OUT OF IT SO THAT YOUR BLESSINGS WILL BE DELAYED.

30 Prayer points Prayers against barrenness *Conceive*

- I break every curse of barrenness upon my life in the name of Jesus Christ.

- Every power of darkness inflicting barrenness upon my life, I bind you in Jesus' name.

- I destroy every cord of barrenness tied around my marriage and family in Jesus' name.

- I revoke every ancestral covenant of barrenness in my family and marriage in Jesus' name.

- I nullify every covenant of barrenness operating in my marriage originating from my family side or from my spouse' family side in the name of Jesus Christ

- The Word of God says, "Whatsoever I shall bind on earth shall be bound in heaven; and whatsoever I shall loose on earth shall be loosed in heaven." (Matt. 18:18 KJV).

- Therefore, I bind and destroy every seed, root, shoot or fruit of barrenness in my life and marriage in Jesus' name.

- I loose upon my life and marriage all of God's blessings of fruitfulness in the name of Jesus Christ.

- Every evil river drowning my life and marriage in barrenness and unfruitfulness, dry up in Jesus' name.

- I destroy by fire, every buried or hidden object, sustaining barrenness in my life and marriage in the name of Jesus Christ.

- I am fruitful in every way; according to the Word of God in Jesus' name.

- Father, bless me with good and healthy children in Jesus' name.

- My womb is fertile and reproductive in Jesus' name.

- My reproductive system is healed and restored in Jesus' name.

- I refuse to agree with every decree holding me bound in the city of barrenness and unfruitfulness in the name of Jesus Christ.

- I release the children God Almighty has given to me, to come forth into the physical through me in Jesus' name.

- 32. Every gates holding back my children from being born, I destroy by fire in the name of Jesus Christ.

- Father, I pray You restore every part in me that has been tampered with or negatively affected; and has brought barrenness upon me in Jesus' name. Lord, heal me totally.

- It is written, ".by the stripes of Jesus Christ, I am healed." (2Pet. 2:24) I receive total healing and restoration upon my body and reproductive system in Jesus' name.

- **Father, in Your Holy Word, no-one who truly serve You, remained neither barren nor unfruitful. My God, I cannot remain barren anymore in Jesus' name.**

- **I refuse from my life and marriage every form of barrenness and infertility in the name of Jesus Christ.**

- **I destroy every powers of darkness or personality causing miscarriage in my life and marriage in Jesus' name.**

- **I reject miscarriage from my life and marriage in Jesus' name.**

- **I shall conceive and give birth naturally, in due season, in the name of Jesus Christ.**

- **Every evil power assigned to attack my pregnancy; I wipe you out of existence, in Jesus' name.**

- **Every person, powers or personalities that agreed that I will never be pregnant nor give birth to children in my lifetime; I command the Holy Ghost fire to destroy you all in Jesus' name.**

- **Every demonic projection into my womb causing infertility, I uproot destroy you in Jesus' name.**

- **Every household wickedness that refuses to release my fruitfulness, I break you asunder in Jesus' name.**

- **Every household wickedness inflicting barrenness upon my marriage, either from my family side or from my spouse's family** side, I bind and destroy you and your works in the name of Jesus Christ.

- Every satanic contraceptive the enemy has inserted into my reproductive organ, I command it to be uprooted and destroyed by fire in Jesus' name.

Day Eight
Tues 8/16/16

Before you pray please follow the instructions below.

a. **Read the Bible Passage below**

   Joshua 1 vs 3

a. **Confess all your sins, both known and unknown**

30 Prayer Points for Restoration/Possessing Your Possessions

- I decree that every word that come out of my mouth as I pray today must be fulfilled in Jesus' name.

- I release the favor of God upon my life in Jesus' name.

- I receive the anointing of restoration in Jesus' name.

- I command total restoration of all things I have lost in Jesus' name.

- Every person or personality who has taken what belongs to me; I command them to release it in Jesus' name. *Restore 100 fold Now*

- I bind and cast out every strong man in my life, family or environment who refuses to release my blessings, breakthrough, miracle, promotion or prosperity in Jesus' name. *ministry, Health, Nephews, House*

- I retrieve back from the hands of the enemy any of my possession that I unknowingly misplaced, in Jesus' name. *(or lost)*

- I command seven-fold restoration of everything the enemy has taken from me, in Jesus' name.

- Oh LORD, restore my wasted years in Jesus' name.

- LORD, restore my wasted efforts, money, health, strength and blessings, in Jesus' name.

- I remove from my life by fire every barrier to my breakthroughs in Jesus' name.

- I uproot and destroy from my life by the Holy Ghost fire every obstacle to my miracle, in Jesus' name.

- I break in pieces every horn scattering my blessings, in the name of Jesus Christ.

- I destroy every hedge the enemy has put over my blessings to prevent me from receiving them in my lifetime, in Jesus' name.

- Every evil power holding back my prayers, or the answers to my prayer, I command you to be bound, in Jesus' name. *with hot chains*

- I release my helper to come to me now, in Jesus' name.

- Every shadow of darkness the enemy has cast over me, to prevent my prosperity, job, business contacts, promotion, or breakthrough from locating me, I remove it by fire, in the name of Jesus Christ.

- I decree total destruction upon every personality that has vowed never to release to me anything God has destined for me, in Jesus' name.

- I break in pieces every covenant or curse obstructing divine restoration in my life, in Jesus' name.

- With the blood of Jesus Christ, I shatter every covenant that gives the enemy upper hand to take from me the blessings God has given to me, in the name of Jesus Christ.

- Every household wickedness eating up the blessings God Almighty has bestowed upon my life and family, I destroy you, in Jesus' name.

- I command a hundred-fold restoration of everything the enemy took from me when I was weak, in Jesus' name.

- I destroy by fire all the horns assigned to scatter my prosperity, family, business and possessions, in Jesus' name.

- I demolish every stumbling block on my way to success, promotion and victory, in Jesus' name.

- Every good thing God has destined for me, but is in the possession of someone else, I command it to come to me now, in Jesus' name.

- Father, I pray, remove any person or personality sitting on my blessings, miracles, breakthrough, prosperity, finance, job or good health, in the name of Jesus Christ.

- I command my blessings and possessions to come to me from wherever they are now, in Jesus' name.

- All my possessions in the north, south, east or west, I command them to come to me now, in Jesus' name.

- All my possessions in the spirit realm, I release them into the physical by fire, in the name of Jesus Christ.

- I receive a hundred-fold restoration of all I have lost, in Jesus' name.

- I receive a hundred-fold restoration of everything the enemy stole from me, in the name of Jesus Christ.

Repeat (handwritten, red)

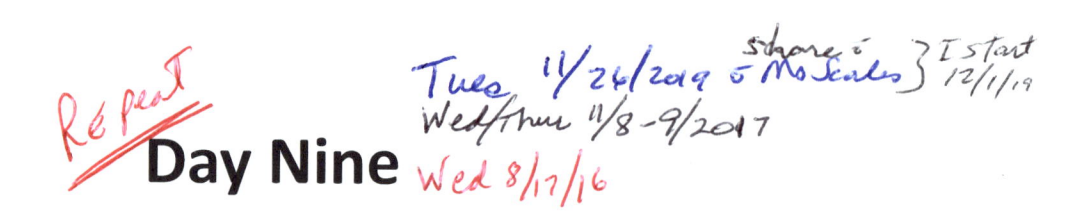

Day Nine

Handwritten annotations: Tues 11/26/2019 share i 5 Mo seals — I start 12/1/19 · Wed/Thur 11/8-9/2017 · Wed 8/17/16

Before you pray please follow the instructions below.

  a. Read the following Bible Passages

  Psalm 115:14, Deuteronomy 8:18

  b. Confess all your sins, both known and unknown

29 Prayer Points for Financial Restoration

- I repent of all financial unfaithfulness in my life. Father, please forgive me.

- Father God I thank You for giving me the wisdom to make wealth in Jesus' name.

- (circled) I seal up totally every spiritual hole the enemy has dug in my pulse, wallet, money bag or account in Jesus' name.

- Every instrument of the enemy designed to bring me down financially, I destroy in Jesus' name.

- I destroy by fire every means the enemy has been using to siphon my finances in Jesus' name.

Handwritten: May the Lord give you increase more and more, you and your children. Psalm 115:14

- I uproot and destroy every hindrance to my financial prosperity and increase in Jesus' name.

- Every wrong deal, contract or contact designed to waste my money, reject in the name of Jesus Christ.

- Every person or personality holding back my financial expansion and multiplication, I command you to loose your hold and be broken in pieces in Jesus' name.

- Every evil money given to me causing a hindrance in my finances, I wipe you out of existence with the Holy Ghost fire, in Jesus' name.

- Every person or personality sent to steal my finance, I send you back empty-handed to your senders; for total destruction in Jesus' name.

- I break and destroy every stronghold over my financial increase in Jesus' name.

- The money I gave out to someone and it was used against me; I reject it and its effects in Jesus' name.

- I command money to locate me now in Jesus' name.

- I receive a hundred-fold restoration of all my wasted finances in the name of Jesus Christ.

- Every imagination of the wicked concerning my finances, I destroy in Jesus' name.

- Every odd job or business designed to distract me from my God-destined financial exploits, I reject, in Jesus' name.

- I destroy from my life every seed of poverty and lack, in Jesus' name.
- Every tree producing bad fruits against my financial dominion, I uproot and consume with the Holy Ghost fire, in Jesus' name.
- I open every financial gate closed against me, by fire, in Jesus' name.
- I receive financial breakthrough in Jesus' name.
- I command every financial pitfall the enemy has dug for me to be covered, in Jesus' name.
- Every foundation of wickedness negating my financial release be destroyed by fire, in Jesus' name.
- Any power causing delay in my life (mention the area that you know you are having delay), O Lord destroy them by fire.
- Any thing from my father's house causing delay in my moving forward break into pieces in Jesus Name.
- I silence every power of delay targeted against my life, in the name of Jesus.
- Spirit of delay I am not your candidate, never show up again in my life in Jesus Name Amen
- O Lord bring to naught all evil counselors and counsels against my breakthrough.
- I destroy by fire evil gang up of my enemy deliberating on how to delay my progress in life in Jesus Name Amen
- O Lord coat my name with fire and favor, no more delay in my breakthrough. In The Name of Jesus

- I command anything growing or present in my life contrary to the will of God to die in the name of Jesus.
- I reject delay in progress planted in me by ~~fathers wife~~ my mother and I render all their power useless in the Jesus Name Amen
- I silence every false prophet speaking against my breakthrough in the name of Jesus.
- O Lord slay every false prophet hired against my life to cause delay in breakthrough. in The Name of Jesus
- I command all my imprisoned benefits to be released, in Jesus' name.
- Let the thunder fire of God strike down all demonic strongholds manufacturing delay in my life. in The Name of Jesus
- O Lord anoint me with the power to pursue, overtake and recover my stolen properties from the power of delay. in The Name of Jesus.
- I command the devil to take his legs off my destiny in Jesus' name.
- I command every demonic vehicle loading away my benefits to be paralyzed in the name of Jesus.
- I receive the power to pursue every stubborn pursuer into the Red Sea in The Name of Jesus.

Day Ten *Fri Nov 10, 2017*
Thurs 8/18/16

Before you pray please follow the instructions below.

   a. **Read the Bible Passage below**

   Colossians 3:5

   a. **Confess all your sins, both known and unknown**

   b. **THINKING OF SEX EVERY TIME WILL DELAY AND DETAINED YOUR BLESSINGS. YOU NEED TO PRAY THE BELOW 44 PRAYER POINTS FOR OVERCOMING SEXUAL STRONGHOLD. THE ENEMIES USE THIS TO DELAY YOUR BLESSINGS.**

44 PRAYER FOR OVERCOMING SEXUAL STRONGHOLD

1 John 1:9; James 5:16; Romans 6:12-18; 1 Corinthians 6:9-20; 2 Corinthians 7:1; Galatians 5:16-23; Colossians 3:5; 1 Thessalonians 4:3-5; 2 Timothy 2:22; Hebrews 13:4

- Heavenly Father, I thank You for the blessings that have come down to me from my ancestors on my father's line and my mother's line.

- But I also acknowledge that as a result of their sinful beliefs and practices, they had also sinned against you in many ways.

- Today I choose to forgive my ancestors for the consequences of their sexual sins that have affected me.

- Please break the yoke and power of this generational curse of sexual sins off me. *Now in The Name of Jesus*

- Please forgive me too for my own sexual sins. *in The Name of Jesus*

- I know I am enslaved to these sins and that I am powerless to deliver myself. *Lord I need you Now in The Name of Jesus.*

- I acknowledge that You can help me and that Jesus have already paid the debt for my sin. *by the shedding of His Blood in The Name of Jesus.*

- All I need to do is claim it personally, for Jesus, had bore all of my sins, past, present and future when He died for me on the cross. *in The Name of Jesus*

- I accept the gift of grace offered to me through Jesus' sacrificial death. *in The Name of Jesus*

- I thank You that You know everything about me. Help me to be completely truthful with You. I don't need to hide any more. *Lord I come to you Transparent, humble*

- ⦿ If I confess my sins, You are faithful and just and will forgive my sins and purify me from all unrighteousness (1 John 1:9).

- Father, You sent Jesus to rescue me from this body of death!

- I don't have to be a prisoner to sin. This battle that rages over my body originates in my mind making me a slave to the sin that is still at work within me.

- Right now, I surrender my mind to You.

- Please cleanse my mind on the conscious, subconscious and unconscious levels.

- Jesus, please Lord over my mind, my thought patterns (Behavior) and attitudes. in The Name

- You have searched me and You know me. You know when I sit and when I rise; You perceive my thoughts from afar. You discern my going out and my lying down; You are familiar with all my ways (Psalm 139:1-3). *Know This*

- Come and dwell in me, Lord, by Your Holy Spirit, and set me free to live in Your resurrection life.

- Please break the control and manipulation of sexual thoughts and images over my mind, body and sexuality. in The Name of Jesus.

- Please forgive me and set me free from all consequences of my sins.

- Please cleanse me of all defilement of spirit, mind, will, emotions and body. *in The Name of Jesus*

- Cleanse my eyes, ears, hands and sexual organs too. *in The Name of Jesus*

- In Jesus' name, Father, lift off me all sexual spirits of lust. *in The Name of Jesus*

- The reason Jesus appeared was to destroy the devil's work (1 John 3:7-8).

- Lord, I have been a willing party to the devil's work. Thank You that You appeared on this earth to die and be raised again to destroy his work.

- Please destroy the works the devil has accomplished in me and through me. Set me apart for Your work from now on. *in The Name of Jesus*

- According to Your Word, no one who is born of God will continue to sin, because God's seed remains in him (1 John 3:9).

- Please help me to understand and admit that I cannot simply go on and on indefinitely in my sin and claim to belong to You.

- I acknowledge to You that my body was not meant for sexual immorality, but for You, Lord.

  - You were meant to take authority over this body and bring it sanctification and meaning. *In The Name of Jesus.*

  - I know that my body is a member of Christ Himself.

  - I shall not then take the members of Christ and unite them in ungodly sexual relationships, whether real or virtual (1 Cor 6:13-15).

  - I renounce the use of my body as an instrument of unrighteousness and by so doing, ask You to break the sexual stronghold that the devil has brought into my life.

- Please help me to exercise Godly control over my sexual urges.

- I have simply misused my body. Please cleanse it for Your use.

- I present my body to You as a living sacrifice, holy and acceptable to You and I choose to reserve the sexual use of my body only with my spouse.

- In Jesus' name, I renounce the lie of the devil that my body is not clean.

- Father, I thank You that You have totally cleansed me unconditionally. *in The Name of Jesus*

- Jesus please Lord over my body and my bodily appetites, my sexuality and sexual expressions.

- Therefore, I can now accept myself. And I choose to accept myself and my body as cleansed, in Jesus' name.

> I know that my body is a temple of the Holy Spirit, who is in me, whom I have received from You. I am not my own; I was bought at a price. Therefore please help me to honour You with my body (1 Corinthians 6:19-20).

> Since I have been raised with Christ, help me to set my heart on things above, where Christ is seated at Your right hand, not on earthly things (Colossians 3:1).

> Please take my passions and redirect them first toward You. Be the chief focus of all my passions and create a new heart within me. In Jesus' name. Amen!

Day Eleven Fri 8/19/16

Before you pray please follow the instructions below.

a. **Read the Bible Passage below**

   1 Kings 11:28

b. Confess all your sins, both known and unknown

30 Prayer Points for delay promotion

✶ I destroy every meeting of witchcraft deliberating on how they will delay my God given promotion in Jesus Name.

✶ O Lord sends confusion and frustration into the camp of my enemy in Jesus Name

✶ O Lord renders the power of my enemies useless in Jesus Name. *Null, void, powerless of No EFFECT.*

✶ I release myself from every association that is ministering disfavor into my life.

✶ I reject and repent from any lifestyle that makes me to stink in the nostrils of God.

✶ 6. Lord, baptize me with the spirit of grace and supplication and favour. *in The Name of Jesus*

7. I reject the spirit of rejection, disfavor and hatred in Jesus name.

8. You seed of generational rejection and disfavor, die in my life in Jesus name.

9. Lord, perfume my life with your oil of favour. *in The Name of Jesus.*

10. Thou favour of God upon my life, begin to displace people for my sake. *in The Name of Jesus*

** 11. Favour of God, create strategic vacancies for me. *Now in The Name of Jesus*

12. You foundational spirit of hatred and rejection in my life, die right now in Jesus name.

13. Every seed of witchcraft in my life; die by fire. *in The Name of Jesus*

14. I command every representation and mark of rejection in my life to burn and perish. *Now in The Name of Jesus*

15. Every seed of rejection, hatred and failure in my life, I command you to be consumed. by the fire of God in the name of Jesus.

16. Every curse, spell, jinx, and enchantment of disfavour in my life, whether acquired, inherited, ancestral or environmental, be destroy from my foundation in Jesus mighty name.

17. Every spirit servicing and enforcing disfavour, rejection and hatred in my life: be bound and liquidated by God's fire in Jesus name.

18. Let the fire and thunder of God visit my foundations on both maternal and paternal sides. in The Name of Jesus

19. All you invisible marks and labels of rejection and disfavour on any part of my body, be blotted out by the blood of Jesus. in The Name of Jesus

20. Father, from henceforth, turn my disgrace into grace, my shame to fame, my labour to favour, my story to glory, my pressure to pleasure and my pain to gain in Jesus name.

21. Every area of my life that I have lost to failure, I command to be restored in Jesus name. → 100 fold.

22. You spirits of rejection and hatred, loose your grip over my life in the name of Jesus.

23. It is written of me that because I meditate in God's Word and seek to do His will, anything I lay my hands upon shall succeed. Therefore, I reject the spirit of failure in any area of my life. I am a success in life, ¬in my profession, in my career, in my business, and in my marriage. Others might have failed, but I believe in a God that cannot fail. I am His child. I am working in partnership with Him. Because He is on my side, I will not be a failure any more in Jesus name.

24. I command all my buried goodness, progress and prosperity to begin to resurrect in the mighty name of Jesus.

25. Father, I am a child of love, grace and favour; therefore, I refuse any form of rejection in Jesus name.

26. I break any spell, curse, jinx, and enchantment of failure and rejection in my life right now in Jesus name.

27. Father, perfume my life with the aroma of Christ, so that from now on good and helpful people will be attracted to me in Jesus name.

28. Holy Spirit, I enter into Your divine favour today. Let the oil of Your favour begin to flow upon me. Everywhere I turn, let the doors be opened to me. Whatever I lay my hands upon, let them succeed in the name of the Lord Jesus.

29. Father from now on, make it impossible for anybody to say no to my sincere requests in Jesus name.

30. Father, give everyone on any panel or committee that will decide my case or cause a special favour and liking for me in Jesus name.

I received pink feather when I was leaving for work.

Day Twelve *Sat 8/20/16*

Before you pray please follow the instructions below.

a. **Read the following Bible Passages**

   Daniel 6:3 Daniel 5:12

b. **Confess all your sins, both known and unknown**

30 PRAYER POINTS for Excellence 1

- Lord, bring honey out of the rock for me this year. in The Name of Jesus

- Lord, open up all the good doors of my life that household wickedness has shut.

- Let all anti- breakthrough designs against my life be shattered to irreparable pieces in the name of Jesus.

- I paralyze all satanic antagonism against my destiny from the womb in the name of Jesus.

- Lord, enlarge my coast beyond my wildest dream in the name of Jesus.

- I claim back all my goods presently residing in wrong hands in the name of Jesus.

- O Lord, uproot evil things that are against my advancement from my life.

- O Lord, plant good things that will advance my cause into my life.

- Let every spiritual weakness in my life receive permanent termination in the name of Jesus.

- Let every financial failure in my life receive permanent termination in the name of Jesus.

- I challenge my problem with the fire of God and blood of Jesus.

- Let every pollution in my life be nullifies by the blood of Jesus.

- Let every evil gathering planning for my downfall be scattered to desolation in Jesus name.

- Let every demonic manipulation aimed at changing my destiny be frustrated in Jesus name.

- Every multiple strongman attached to my life, be paralyzed and die in the name of Jesus.

- Let every demonic power local or international power doing night vigil because of me be scattered by the stones of fire in the name of Jesus.

- I challenge every spiritual poison in my body with Holy Ghost fire and command their ejection in Jesus name.

- I receive strength to do that which my enemies say is impossible in the name of Jesus.

- Every goodness of mine that has been spiritually swallowed should be released in Jesus name.

- I command every power prolonging any battle in my life to receive permanent defeat in the name of Jesus.

- I command the strangers to depart from the house of my life in Jesus name.

- I ask you father in the name of Jesus to send your angels to cause me to come into my treasury everything the Enemy has stolen or confiscated from me be restored 100 fold Now in The Name of Jesus.

- The promises of God will not fail upon my life in the name of Jesus.

- I release myself today from every demonic trap in Jesus name.

- I decree confusion into the camp of the oppressors. in The Name of Jesus

- Any power given the mandate to curse and hinder my progress, summersault and die, in the name of Jesus.

- Every agent assigned to frustrate me, perish by fire, in the name of Jesus.

- God, smash me and renew my strength, in the name of Jesus.

- **Lord, ignite my career, business, ministry with Your fire in the name of Jesus.**

- Every evil spiritual padlock and evil chain hindering my success, be roasted, in the name of Jesus.

- Lord, anoint my eyes and my ears that they may see and hear wondrous things from heaven

✱ Day Thirteen Sun 8/21/16

Before you pray please follow the instructions below.

a. Read the Bible Passage below

Philippians 1:9-10

b. Confess all your sins, both known and unknown

30 PRAYER POINTS for Excellence 2

- **Let the blood of Jesus remove any unprogressive label from every aspect of my life, in Jesus' name.**

- In the name of Jesus, I refuse to fear, because God has not given me the spirit of fear, but of power and of love and of a sound mind.

- I bind the spirit of fear in my life, in the name of Jesus.

- I break every evil covenant that has brought fear into my life, in the name of Jesus.

- I command every terror of the night that has brought fear into my life to stop and move from my environment, in the name of Jesus.

- **All negative doors that the spirit of fear has opened in the past, be closed now, in the name of Jesus.**

- Every disease, oppression and depression that came into my life as a result of fear, disappear now, in the name of Jesus.
- This session is titled: Power Against Evil Pattern
- Every plantation of witchcraft in my family, what are you waiting for? Die, in the name of Jesus.
- Every pattern of household witchcraft in my family, I bury you today, in the name of Jesus.
- O God arise, and let every witchcraft power release my destiny, in the name of Jesus.
- Every stronghold of death and tragedy in my family, scatter by fire, in the name of Jesus.
- Every messenger of death operating in my family line, die in the name of Jesus.
- Every garment of evil pattern against my divine goal, roast, in the name of Jesus.

- Every evil pattern of non-achievement in my family clear out now, in the name of Jesus.

- Every giant of almost-there in my family, drop dead, in the name of Jesus.

- You evil pattern of poverty, die, in the name of Jesus.

- The Lord should remove spiritual cataract from my eyes.

- Lord, open up my understanding. *in The Name of Jesus*

- Lord, teach me deep and secret things. *in The Name of Jesus*

- Lord, reveal to me every secret behind any problem that I have. *in The Name of Jesus.*

- Lord, ~~should~~ bring to the light every thing planned against me in darkness.

- The Lord should ignite and revive my beneficial potentials. Now in The Name of Jesus

- I bind every demon that pollutes spiritual vision and dreams in the name of Jesus.

  - Let every dirtiness blocking my communication pipe with the living God be washed clean with the blood of Jesus. in The Name of Jesus

  - I receive power to operate with sharp spiritual eyes that cannot be deceived in the name of Jesus.

  - Let profitable business meet me on the way in Jesus' name.

  - No devourer shall ever destroy the fruit of my labor in Jesus' name.

- You devourers and wasters of fortune, I command you to depart from my life in the name of Jesus.

- I use the Blood of Jesus Christ to wash my hands and my entire body and make them clean today.

- I retrieve my blessings from every evil attack in Jesus' name

Day Fourteen Monday Aug 22, 2016 / Tues 11/14/17

Before you pray please follow the instructions below.

a. **Read the Bible Passage below**

   Colossians 3:23

b. **Confess all your sins, both known and unknown**

30 PRAYER POINTS for Excellence 3

- I break every curse of failure in the name of Jesus.

- Let the spirit of favor be opened upon me everywhere I go concerning my business.

- Father, I ask You in the name of Jesus to send ministering spirits to bring in prosperity into my business.

- Let men bless me Every where I go. in The Name of Jesus

- I release my business from the clutches of financial hunger in the name of Jesus.

- I loose angels in the mighty name of Jesus to go and create favor for my company.

- Let all financial hindrances be removed in Jesus' name.

- Every destiny destroyed by polygamy, be reversed, in the name of Jesus.

- Every witchcraft power working against my destiny, fall down and die, in the name of Jesus.

- Every incantation and ritual working against my destiny, be disgraced, in the name of Jesus.

- Every power of darkness assigned against my destiny, fall down and die, in the name of Jesus.

- Every evil power trying to re-program my life, fall down and die, in the name of Jesus.

- I reject every rearrangement of my destiny by household wickedness, in the name of Jesus.

- Father Lord, let Christ dwell in my heart by faith, in Jesus' name.

- Father Lord, let me be rooted and grounded in love, in Jesus' name

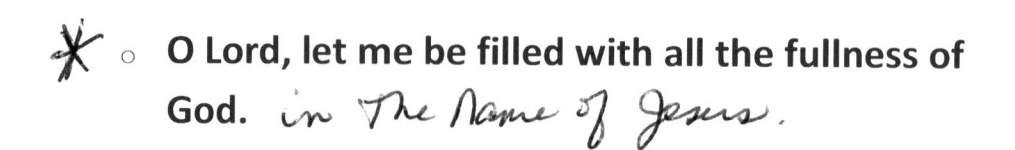

- O Lord, let me be filled with all the fullness of God. in The Name of Jesus.

- Let the word of the Lord have free course and be glorified in me, in the name of Jesus.

- Let the Lord of peace give me peace in all areas of life, in the name of Jesus.

- O Lord, perfect what is lacking in my faith.

- Lord, open doors of opportunity to me through this prayer, in the name of Jesus.

- I recover all the ground that I had lost to the enemy, in Jesus' name

- I command all doors of good things, closed against me by the enemy to be opened, in the name of Jesus.

- I reject the spirit of impossibility, I claim open doors, in the name of Jesus.

- I decree restoration seven fold in ALL . . . areas of my life, in the name of Jesus.

- I posses the power to pursue, overtake and recover my goods from spiritual Egyptians, in Jesus name.

- Lord, make my life a miracle and be glorified in every area of it, in the name of Jesus.

- Let all hidden potentials and gifts that will make me great, stolen from me, be restored 21 fold, in Jesus name.

- Let all security-men in charge of satanic banks that are harboring my blessings be paralyzed, in Jesus name.

- I terminate the appointment of all satanic bankers and managers, in the name of Jesus.

Day Fifteen   *Tues Aug 23, 2016*

Before you pray please follow the instructions below.

   a. **Read the Bible Passage below**

   2 Peter 1:3-4

   b. **Confess all your sins, both known and unknown**

30 PRAYER POINTS for Excellence 4

- I command the thunder of God to break to pieces all the satanic strong-rooms harboring my properties, in Jesus name.

- I possess all my properties, in the name of Jesus.

- Let all satanic instruments used against me be completely destroyed, in Jesus' name.

- I command all satanic clearing houses and agents to be roasted, in the name of Jesus.

- I paralyze completely all satanic transactions and contracts against my life, in the name of Jesus.

- Let all satanic network and computers fashioned against me be disorganized, in the name of Jesus.

- Heavenly Father, let all blood that has been stored up in satanic bank come forth, in the name of Jesus.

- Every spirit of limitation against my breakthroughs, die, in the name of Jesus.

- Every power of demotion targeted against my destiny, die, in the name of Jesus.

- Every spirit, power and personality working against my elevation, die, in the name of Jesus.

- I refuse to carry the evil-left over of my family, in the name of Jesus.

- Every evil standing order against my destiny, die, in the name of Jesus.

- Every ancestral curse working against my destiny, die, in the name of Jesus.

- O God arise and begin to disgrace all my Goliaths, in the name of Jesus.

- Let my Pharaoh die in his own Red Sea, in the name of Jesus.

- I fire back every arrow of spiritual demotion, in the name of Jesus.

- I fire back every arrow of physical demotion, in the name of Jesus.

- I fire back every arrow of financial demotion, in the name of Jesus.

- I fire back every arrow of marital demotion, in the name of Jesus.

- O Lord, plant good things in my life.

- O Lord, uproot evil things from my life.

- I cancel every unconscious negative agreement, in Jesus' name.

- Let every spiritual weakness in my life receive termination now, in the name of Jesus.

- Let every financial failure in my life receive termination now, in the name of Jesus.

- Let every sickness in my life receive termination now, in the name of Jesus.

- Let every architect of problems receive termination now, in the name of Jesus.

- Paralyze all spiritual wolves working against my life, in the name of Jesus.

- Let that which hinders me from greatness begin to give way now, in the mighty name of Jesus.

- Let every imprisoned and buried potentials begin to come forth now, in the name of Jesus.

Day Sixteen *Thurs Nov 16, 2017*
Wed Aug 24, 2016

Before you pray please follow the instructions below.

- a. **Read the Bible Passage below**

    Ephesians 6:7-8

- b. **Confess all your sins, both known and unknown**

30 PRAYER POINTS for Excellence 5

> ➢ **As from today, I receive the power for a new beginning in the name of Jesus.**

- Father, I dedicate and consecrate the works of my hands to you as from today, in the name of Jesus.

- Almighty Father, initiate a hunger and demand for my skills and talents, goods and services in the name of Jesus.

- I use the blood of Jesus to wash my hands and my products/services clean today in Jesus' name.

- O Lord, give me the spirit of favor in all my business transactions in Jesus' name.

Going into The Spirit
Sale of my house
purchase of New house
Financial Debts paid off

- Anything in my life keeping ………… (mention what you want) from coming to me, be destroyed immediately in the name of Jesus.

- Every virtue of my life buried by wicked powers, come out now in the name of Jesus.

- Every wealth stolen from me when I was a baby, I re-possess you now in the name of Jesus.

- O heavens over my finances, open now in the name of Jesus.

- Let wealth jump out of the habitation of the wicked and locate me now in the name of Jesus.

- Angels of poverty, clear away from the gates of my breakthroughs in the name of Jesus.

- Angels of the living God, pursue wealth into my hands in the name of Jesus.

- All the negative effects of my ancestors on my finances, be reversed by the blood of Jesus.

- I put my foot on the ground and I declare that this earth must cooperate with me in the mighty name of Jesus.'

- **Portal angels of God, open the storehouses of God unto me in the name of Jesus.**

- Every power of my father's house working to demote my destiny, die in the name of Jesus.

- Every witchcraft attack at the gate of my breakthrough, be buried now in the name of Jesus.

- Every good thing that anger has stolen from my life, I repossess them now in Jesus' name.

- **I refuse to be discouraged at the edge of my breakthrough in Jesus' name.**

- I refuse to be provoked at the gate of my breakthrough in the name of Jesus.

- I recover my portion from the hands of dead relatives in the mighty name of Jesus.

- All my inheritance that has been transferred to another, I command you to return in the name of Jesus.

- I break the backbone of every spirit of conspiracy and treachery against me in Jesus' name.

- Let the fire of the Lord purge my finances and business from every evil mark in Jesus' name.

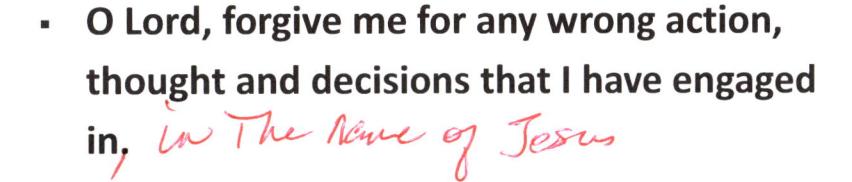

- O Lord, forgive me for any wrong action, thought and decisions that I have engaged in, in The Name of Jesus

- O Lord, open my eyes to see into the spirit in Jesus' name.

- O Lord, give me the wisdom to walk away from satanic traps and snares in Jesus' name.

- I frustrate every satanic verdict against me in the name of Jesus

- Let the finger, terror, anger, fear, wrath, hatred and burning judgment of God be released upon my fulltime enemies in the name of Jesus

- Every power preventing the perfect will of God from happening in my life, receive failure and defeat in Jesus' name.

Day Seventeen *Thurs Aug 25, 2016*

Before you pray please follow the instructions below.

a. **Read the Bible Passage below**

   2 Corinthians 8:7

b. **Confess all your sins, both known and unknown**

30 PRAYER POINTS for Excellence 6

- Let the warring angels and the Spirit of God arise and scatter every evil gathering sponsored against me in Jesus' name

- I disobey every satanic order programmed by inheritance into my life, in the name of Jesus

- I bind and cast out any power causing <u>internal warfare</u> in my life, in the name of Jesus

- Every demonic doorkeeper locking out good things against me, be paralyzed by fire in the name of Jesus

- I command every evil power fighting me to turn around and fight against themselves till they are all <u>destroyed</u> in the name of Jesus

Pray With Power Along With all you claim Now

- Every demon hindering, delaying, preventing, or destroying my breakthroughs, I order you into the pit in the name of Jesus

- I command civil war in the kingdom of my enemies in the name of Jesus

- I receive the power to get wealth in the name of Jesus.

Handwritten margin notes (left):
- Head full of Hair - manageable
- Supernatural weight loss
- Financial Freedom
- All Bills/debts paid in full
- Knowledge
- Wisdom
- Understanding
- Truth
- Fear of the Lord
- Discernment
- Might/Power
- Book of my Life
- Eyes to see my Angels
- Ability to work w/ my Angels
- Hunger + Thirst for The Lord
- Creative Ideas
- Powerful Books written by Holy Spirit through me

- In the mighty name of Jesus, I claim…. (pick from the following)

Handwritten margin notes (right): Isaiah 45:1-3 — Heaven on Earth, Pursuit of Lord
- My God given dreams
- My God given potentials
- The Spirit of the Lord on me
- My New Luxury Furnished home Paid in full
- All Spiritual Blessings
- All Spiritual Gifts
- Eyes to See / Ears to hear
- Ability to go to Throne Room, Heaven, Spirit Realm

- O LORD, by all the power for which you are known to be God, let my prosperity appear in the name of Jesus.

- My Father and my LORD, I thank you for answering these prayers in Jesus name.

- I bind every anti-open door demon around me in Jesus Christ Name, Amen!

- By thunder, I burst open every closed doors to my success now in Jesus Christ Name, Amen!

- Lord, I ask for open doors in my business, all to Your glory in Christ Jesus, Amen!

- I receive spiritual open doors by fire in Jesus Christ Name, Amen!

- I receive the power to make and get wealth in Jesus Christ Name, Amen!

- I ask for open doors into the nations in Jesus Christ Name, Amen!

- I receive open doors testimonies in my career, job, marriage and ministry henceforth in Jesus Christ Name, Amen!

- My Father, hold my right hand to open doors that cannot be shut by the enemies henceforth in Jesus Christ Name, Amen (Isaiah 45:1)

- This year is my year of unusual greatness. Therefore LORD! Open unto me unusual doors of greatness that cannot be shut again in Jesus Christ Name, Amen!

- I enter O LORD, into my all round open doors and divine financial breakthroughs by fire now in Jesus Christ Name, Amen!

- Thank God for the name of Jesus.
- Lord, open doors of opportunity to me through this prayer, in the name of Jesus.
- I command all evil unknown forces organised against my life to be scattered, in the name of Jesus.
- I paralyse every activity of physical and spiritual parasites and devourers in my life, in the name of Jesus.
- Powers denying me my due miracles, receive the stones of fire, in the name of Jesus.
- I recover all the ground that I had lost to the enemy, in Jesus' name
- I bind the spirit of depression, frustration and disillusionment in my life, in the name of Jesus.
- Heavenly surgeons, perform the necessary surgical operations in all the areas of my life, in the name of Jesus.
- Lord Jesus, carry out all the repairs that are necessary in my life. Decree aggressively

Day Eighteen Fri Aug 26, 2016

Before you pray please follow the instructions below.

   a. **Read the Bible Passage below**

   Psalms 119:99

   b. **Confess all your sins, both known and unknown**

20 PRAYER POINTS for Excellence 7

- Let all the parasites feeding on any area of my life be roasted, in the name of Jesus.
- Fire of God, consume the evil clock of the enemy that is working against my life, in the name of Jesus.
- My life is not a fertile ground for any evil to thrive in, Jesus' name.
- I command all doors of good things, closed against me by the enemy to be opened, in the name of Jesus.

- I reject the spirit of impossibility, I claim open doors, in the name of Jesus.

- I decree restoration seven fold in . . . areas of my life, in the name of Jesus.

  all spiritual blessing
  sale of House
  Finances
  ministry
  health
  Business

- I refuse to wage war against myself, in the name of Jesus.

- Lord, make my case a miracle. Shock my foes, friends, and even myself, in the name of Jesus.

- Lord, give me the solution to any problem facing me, in the name of Jesus.

- Trees of problems in my life, dry up to the roots, in Jesus' name.

- Walls of physical and spiritual opposition, fall after the order of Jericho, in the name of Jesus.

- Let my king Uzziah die, so that I can see Your face, O Lord, in the name of Jesus.

- I posses the power to pursue, overtake and recover my goods from spiritual Egyptians, in the name of Jesus.

- Let every spell, jinxes, and demonic incantations rendered against me be cancelled, in the name of Jesus.

- I cancel every effect of any strange help received from Egypt regarding this problem, in the name of Jesus.

- Lord, heal all wounds and spiritual bullets sustained from attacks of the enemy.

- Let all hidden potentials and gifts that will make me great, stolen from me, be restored 21 fold, in the name of Jesus.
- I reject the spirit of regret, woes and disappointment, in the name of Jesus.
- Lord, give me power for a new beginning.
- Lord, make my life a miracle and be glorified in every area of it, in the name of Jesus.
- Lord Jesus, I thank You for answering my prayer.

Day Nineteen Sat Aug 27, 2016

Before you pray please follow the instructions below.

a. Read the following Bible Passages

b. Deuteronomy 28:1-14, 8:18

c. Confess all your sins, both known and unknown

30 Prayer points for uncommon breakthroughs

1. Defeat, I defeat you by the power in the blood of Jesus. *in The name of Jesus.*

2. Enough is enough. I posses my possession by fire, in the name of Jesus.

3. Every power troubling my dream, my God shall trouble you today, in the name of Jesus.

4. Every curse with long legs, in my family, die, in the name of Jesus.

5. My enemies, my problems are over, it is now your turn, therefore, carry your loads, in the name of Jesus.

6. Every darkness hanging on my family tree, be broken, in the name of Jesus.

7. Anointing to disgrace my problems, fall on me, in the name of Jesus.

8. Yokes of satanic delay, break, in the name of Jesus.

9. Any power falling asleep to harm me, you shall not wake up, in the name of Jesus.

10. I break the coffin of darkness by the hammer of fire, in the name of Jesus.

11. Vultures of darkness, assigned against me, die, in the name of Jesus.

Spirit of The Lord
Wisdom
Discernment / understanding
Counsel
Might
Knowledge
reverential fear of The Lord

12. Seven spirits of God, manifest in my life, in the name of Jesus. (Isa. 11:2)

13. Every power that wants me to suffer what my parents suffered, die, in the name of Jesus.

14. Every financial grave dug for me, scatter, in the name of Jesus.

15. Any problem associated with any dead relative, die, in the name of Jesus.

16. I jump over the plan of the enemy to kill me, in the name of Jesus.

17. Fake doors, opened by the enemy for me, close, in the name of Jesus.

18. Storms of life, shut up by fire, in the name of Jesus.

19. Every poison in my body, die, in the name of Jesus.

20. Let men + women begin to compete to favour me, in the name of Jesus.

21. Satanic prophets summoning my spirit, receive madness, in the name of Jesus.

22. Satanic siren, scarring away my prosperity, shut up, in the name of Jesus.

23. Every power of useless investment, die, in the name of Jesus.

24. Anything burned to harm my destiny, catch fire, in the name of Jesus.

25. O God of signs and wonders, appear in my situation by fire, in the name of Jesus.

26. Fingers of the wicked, harassing my breakthroughs, wither, in the name of Jesus.

27. O God, arise and hiss over my enemies, in the name of Jesus.

28. Every vampire power, assigned against me, die, in the name of Jesus.

29. Thunder of God, arise, waste my enemies, in the name of Jesus.

(30.) Thou power of the strongman, blocking my chances, die, in the name of Jesus.

Day Twenty *Sun Aug 28, 2016*

Before you pray please follow the instructions below.

a. **Read the following Bible Passages**

   Proverbs 10:4, 22:29

b. **Confess all your sins, both known and unknown**

30 PRAYER POINTS for Uncommon Breakthroughs 2

- Power of delayed blessing, die, in the name of Jesus.

- Every power that wants me to labor in vain, die, in the name of Jesus.

- My investments, arise, magnetize great profits, in the name of Jesus.

- Oh Lord, baptize me with the generous spirit of a cheerful giver who gives out of love and not out of compulsion.

- The Lord will make me a pillar of support for the expansion of God's Kingdom in Jesus name.

- All my past generosity will be remembered by God. Every impossible situation in my life will be turned around by God on the account of my past generosity in Jesus name.

- I believe in miracles, I serve a God of miracles therefore; every chapter closed by men against me will be re-opened by God in my favour in Jesus name.

- Just as the famine in the days of Joseph elevated him, help me Lord to see the opportunity that the current global financial crises is creating for my prosperity in Jesus name

- Oh Lord endow me with the required mental skill to interpret every opportunity that comes my way correctly and take maximum advantage of them in Jesus name.

- I receive Grace to enjoy riches that will endure throughout my life time in Jesus name.

- I receive total liberty from the embarrassing yoke of debt in Jesus name.

- I receive total deliverance from the embarrassing stigma of knocking on doors and repeated phone calls begging for financial assistance in Jesus name.

- I will enjoy the surplus of heaven to achieve my purpose and have leftovers in Jesus name.

- Murmuring will not take the place of money in my life and money will not mess me up, all my bills will be supernaturally settled in Jesus name.

- I refuse to be a burden on my neighbours, families and friends. I am a lender and not a borrower in Jesus name.

- Whenever the needies need my help my purse will not be empty. I will be readily available to meet their needs in Jesus name.

- Oh Lord, deliver me (my husband, my children etc) from the slavery of evil appetite/habit that are killing my health and destiny in Jesus name.

- The Lord will satisfy my mouth with good things. I shall have appetite and money to eat choiced foods and accomplish great things in Jesus name.

- I receive total deliverance from the curse of poverty and affliction that has ever plaqued my family line. I will live to transfer prosperity to my posterity in Jesus name.

- I shall not only be great in wealth but also have great name in Jesus name.

- Let your Spirit empower me oh Lord, to attain, sustain and enjoy success in Jesus name.

- My joy shall multiply at the end of this month... I shall therefore count blessings and not sorrows in Jesus name.

- Oh Lord deliver me from profitless labour and confused activities in Jesus name.

- I shall not waste my seed. I will be divinely guided to plant my seed on fertile soil in Jesus name.

- Oh Lord, let the resources required to fulfill my dream in the custody of my enemies relocate into the custody of my friends and helpers in Jesus name.

- Oh Lord, let money forever remains my loyal messenger in Jesus name.

- Both the help from above and abroad will combine and compete to settle my bills and fulfill my dreams this year in Jesus name.

- From now on all my investments and labour since the beginning of my career and ministry will begin to yield their full profit in Jesus name.

- In every tight situation, let my tithe provoke heavenly solution in Jesus name.

- This week my past generosity will spring forth a pleasant surprise in Jesus name.

Day Twenty One *Mon Aug 29, 2016*

Before you pray please follow the instructions below.

   a. **Read the Bible Passage below**

   Joshua 1:8;

   b. **Confess all your sins, both known and unknown**

30 PRAYER POINTS for Uncommon Breakthroughs 3

- Throughout this year, none of my resources shall be wasted on medical bills or any form of profitless venture in Jesus name.

- Satan will not receive the backing of heaven to wipe out my financial resources with evil erosion in Jesus name.

- Whosoever looks up to me for help this year will not be disappointed. I shall have enough to satisfy my needs and plenty to give to others in need in Jesus name.

  - I receive deliverance from the bondage of doubt and fear that past failures and misfortune has introduced into my life in Jesus name.

  - I receive the required courage to step into the greatness God has ordained for me in Jesus name.

  - I submit to the leadership of God's Spirit and I receive the backing of heaven to breakthrough and succeed in all my undertakings in Jesus name.

- I receive the favourable countenance of God, therefore Heaven will agree with all my steps of faith and God's will shall prosper in my hands.

- I refuse to submit my courage to frustration. God will send me encouragement today; I will be energized to continue the race in Jesus name.

- The sun is rising today announcing my season of success and fulfilling my purpose in Jesus name.

- Those that believe in me and have invested in my dream, encouraging and supporting me will not be disappointed in Jesus name.

- The Lord will allow something better to come out of every bad situation that baffles me in Jesus name.

- Let the prophetic power that operated in the valley of dry bones re-unite me with my lost (glory, helper, husband, wife, children, joy etc) in Jesus name.

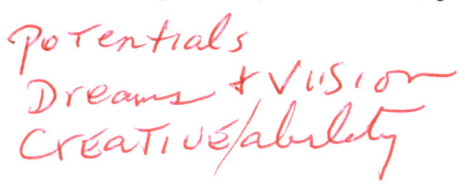

Potentials
Dreams + Vision
Creative ability

- Every carnal attitude of disobedience and demonic spirits that are promoting barrenness in my life are terminated today in Jesus name.

- Those doubting my ability to succeed will soon become my subjects in Jesus name.

- Those that refuse to lend unto me during my moment of struggling will soon begin to lean on me in Jesus name.

- Those laughing at me today will soon laugh with me and regret their folly of looking down on me in Jesus name.

- Those who gather to frustrate my vision will beg to be part of my celebration in Jesus name.

- Every opposition I encounter today will soon form a chapter of my success story in Jesus name.

- The Lord will release a measure of prosperity into my life that will swallow all my history of poverty in Jesus name.

- The Lord will give me a new name and a new identity that will bury all the ugly stories associated with my background in Jesus name.

- My new life in Christ has clothed me with a garment of righteousness; my past sinful life will no longer hurt or haunt me in Jesus name.

- A similar grace that made Jabez more honourable than his brethren will distinguish me among my equals in Jesus name.

- Today marks the beginning of my bouncing back. My spiritual life shall be restored and my lost glory shall be fully recovered.

- I declare every department of my life under the control of Satan disconnected in Jesus name.

- All the sinful habits that enslave me to Satan will henceforth irritate me in Jesus name.

- In all the areas where men have failed me, let your mercy prevail for me in Jesus name.

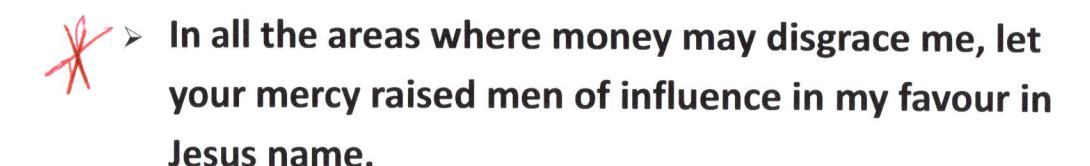

- In all the areas where money may disgrace me, let your mercy raised men of influence in my favour in Jesus name.

- This week I will encounter God's mercy that will end all problems of money associated with my family in Jesus name.

- Inadequate supply will not compel me to abandon God. Excess supply will not deceive me to disconnect from God in Jesus name.

- I receive Christ Spirit of endurance to endure the season of adversity and wait for the era of prosperity in Jesus name.

> The present adversity will not last forever; my business will not sink with the ongoing economic meltdown. The Spirit of God will usher in a new era of prosperity in Jesus name.

Day Twenty Two *Tues Aug 30, 2016*

Before you pray please follow the instructions below.

a. **Read the Bible Passage below**

   Ecclesiastes 5:19.

b. **Confess all your sins, both known and unknown**

30 PRAYER POINTS for Uncommon Breakthroughs 4

- God's covenant of exception as it was in the land of Goshen will work in my favour against the ongoing economic recession in Jesus name.

- Whatever positive purpose, I pursue, I will posses because the Spirit of God will instruct my steps in the right direction in Jesus name.

- I rebuke the spirit of bareness from my business; my business will be fruitful and profitable in Jesus name.

- The Holy Spirit will be the invincible Chief Executive Officer of my business in Jesus name.

- I will not suffer scarcity of idea nor adequate capital to take my business to the next level in Jesus name.

- The Spirit of God will expose and expel every Achan (traitor) among my employees that has the tendency of ruining my business in Jesus name.

- The Spirit of God will deliver me from making recruitment error that is capable of crippling my business in Jesus name.

- The Spirit of excellence, commitment, loyalty and uprightness will compel all my employees to work for the progress of my company in Jesus name.

- Evil intentions and machination of my competitors will fail in Jesus name.

- Every weapon sponsored through family relations or friends to wreck my business will not succeed in Jesus name.

- I pronounce unstoppable prosperity over every project of my company in Jesus name.

- 70. Because this business is founded in partnership with God, it will take root downward, develop into branches and bear fruits upward in Jesus name.

- I command a miraculous and total recovery of all debts owned my company in Jesus name.

- All my long-forgotten proposal will begin to receive the attention of the right and relevant authority in Jesus name.

- The favour of God will envelope my company, office and shop in Jesus name.

- Both my company identity and complimentary card will carry God's presence and attract favour of my prospective customers, clients and contracts in Jesus name.

- I repeal every Local and International legislation that is not in favour of the prosperity of my business in Jesus name.

- My business premises will not receive demonic visitation of armed robbers and dupes; law enforcement agents sponsored against me will not succeed at implicating me in Jesus name.

- Partnership that will ruin my business will not receive my endorsement in Jesus name.

- Agent of darkness on evil assignment against my business will receive God's judgment of blindness in Jesus name.

- The economic policy of this nation will begin to favour the prosperity of my business in Jesus name.

- The vision of the Government in power will not antagonize my business prosperity in Jesus name.

- Anoint me Lord to breakthrough without bribery in Jesus name.

- Holy Ghost fire will consume all satanic rope and chains that is around my wrongly seized goods; heaven will secure their release this week in Jesus name.

- I untie all my customers and clients that have been tied around the aprons of my competitors with demonic spell in Jesus name.

- Every goods that have overstayed in this shop and are at the risk of expiration will bring in money and relocate to its end users (consumer) in Jesus name.

- This month I will sign a contract whose profit will pay all my debts and leave me with surplus that will make me to have nothing to do with debt again in Jesus name.

- This month, my business premises will relocate from a rented apartment to our own property in Jesus name.

- Henceforth, I will not borrow to pay my staff again in Jesus name.

- My business will be sufficient to pay my bills, pay my staff and surplus enough to contribute to community development in Jesus name.

Day Twenty Three *Wed Aug 31, 2016*

Before you pray please follow the instructions below.

   a. **Read the Bible Passage below**

   Psalms 89:1

   b. **Confess all your sins, both known and unknown**

30 PRAYER POINTS for Uncommon Breakthroughs 5

- I receive help from above to resurrect my collapse business and expand and diversify my flourishing ones in Jesus name.

- I will not lack creative ideas to satisfy my customers / clients in Jesus name.

- All the customers that I have pursued in the past without success will begin to beg to do business with me in Jesus name.

- The current economic meltdown will not fold up my business in Jesus name.

- The winnowing power of God's Spirit will blow away the spirit of waste and agents of waste from my business in Jesus name.

- God's wind of wonder will deposit wealth into my business in Jesus name.

- ➢ The Spirit of God will guide my business decision; my capital shall not be tied down on unprofitable goods in Jesus name.

- ➢ Products that have lost market value, and customers taste and appetite will not be grounded in my shop in Jesus name.

- ➢ The Spirit of God will resist me from being teleguided or manipulated by fraudsters (419) to sign away all that I have labored for in Jesus name.

- ➢ I shall not be manipulated by greed and covetousness to disobey heavenly warning through dream and prophecy in Jesus name.

- ➢ None of my business trips will record arm robbery attack or accident in Jesus name.

- ➢ The supreme council of heaven will repeal, reverse, and amend every decree, policy, legislation that is contrary to all my noble business vision in Jesus name.

- Father Lord, by your mighty power, by the power in the Blood of Jesus, Fire of Holy Ghost, scatter and destroy any hindering spirit around me, in the name of Jesus.

- Father Lord, scatter and destroy the power of devouring spirit and limitation, in the name of Jesus.

- Father Lord, any decree made upon my feet because I have come to Christ, let it be revoked in Jesus' name.

- Father Lord, let my feet be anointed and washed by your blood to lead me to peaceful places, in the name of Jesus.

- Father Lord, release the spirit of carpenter upon me to destroy the horns of enemies, in the name of Jesus.

- Any decree to cause satanic road-block in my way of breakthrough, be scattered by fire, in the name of Jesus.

- Father Lord, come and be our shepherd, to keep us together and save us from thieves, in Jesus' name.

- Every satanic or collective power that wants to scatter what I have gathered, I command you to fall down and die, in the name of Jesus.

- Association of evil gang-up or witchcraft power to cause derailment in my life; scatter by Fire, in the name of Jesus.

- Any power put in place to supervise and confirm failure in my life, die by Fire, in the name of Jesus.

- Anything in me contradicting the word of God to cause error, die by Fire, in the name of Jesus.

- Any power making a decree to affect my standing in the Lord, break by fire, in the name of Jesus.

- Evil decree or curse over my life, spiritually, physically, financially, matrimonially and educationally, I break you, in the name of Jesus.

- Anything in me, around me, within me, contesting with the presence of Holy Spirit in me, are you still alive? die forever and perish, in the name of Jesus.

- Spirit of the Living God, arise and take me to my place of blessing now, in Jesus name.

- Father Lord, whatever weapon or tricks of the enemy to steal, kill and destroy, destroy them with their weapon forever, in Jesus name.

- Father Lord, connect, correct and direct my helpers to me anywhere, anywhere they may be, in the name of Jesus.

- Spirit of the Living God, arise and remove any evil veil covering my face so I can see in Jesus name.

- Power to succeed in life, come upon me now, in the name of Jesus.

- ➢ Power to see and discern, come upon me, in the name of Jesus.

- ➢ Power to over-come, fall upon me now, in the name of Jesus.

Day Twenty Four *Thurs Sept 1, 2016*

Before you pray please follow the instructions below.

Generational Curses can delay or detained your Blessing if they are not addressed

a. **Read the following Bible Passages**

   Numbers 14:18. Galatians 3:13

b. **Confess all your sins, both known and unknown**

25 PRAYER POINTS for Breaking of Generational Curses

- I break all generational curses of pride, rebellion, lust, poverty, witchcraft, idolatry, death, destruction, failure, sickness, infirmity, fear, schizophrenia, and rejection in the name of Jesus.

- I command all generational and hereditary spirits operating in my life through curses to be bound and cast out in the name of Jesus.

- I command all spirits of lust, perversion, adultery, fornication, uncleanness, and immorality to come out of my sexual character in the name of Jesus.

- I command all spirits of hurt, rejection, fear, anger, wrath, sadness, depression, discouragement, grief, bitterness, and unforgiveness to come out of my emotions in the name of Jesus.

- I command all spirits of confusion, forgetfulness, mind control, mental illness, double-mindedness, fantasy, pain, pride, and memory recall to come out of my mind in the name of Jesus.

- I break all curses of schizophrenia and command all spirits of double-mindedness, rejection, rebellion, and root of bitterness to come out in the name of Jesus.

- I command all spirits of guilt, shame, and condemnation to come out of my conscience in the name of Jesus.

- I command all spirits of pride, stubbornness, disobedience, rebellion, self-will, selfishness, and arrogance to come out of my will in the name of Jesus.

- I command all spirits of addiction to come out of my appetite in the name of Jesus.

- I command all spirits of witchcraft, sorcery, divination, and occult to come out in the name of Jesus.

- I command all spirits operating in my head, eyes, mouth, tongue, and throat to come out in the name of Jesus.

- I command all spirits operating in my chest and lungs to come out in the name of Jesus.

- I command all spirits operating in my back and spine to come out in the name of Jesus.

- I command all spirits operating in my stomach, navel, and abdomen to come out in the name of Jesus.

- I command all spirits operating in my heart, spleen, kidneys, liver, and pancreas to come out in the name of Jesus.

- I command all spirits operating in my sexual organs to come out in the name of Jesus.

- I command all spirits operating in my hands, arms, legs, and feet to come out in the name of Jesus.

- I command all demons operating in my skeletal system, including my bones, joints, knees, and elbows, to come out in the name of Jesus.

- I command all spirits operating in my glands and endocrine system to come out in the name of Jesus.

- I command all spirits operating in my blood and circulatory systems to come out in the name of Jesus.

- I command all spirits operating in my muscles and muscular system to come out in the name of Jesus.

- I command all religious spirits of doubt, unbelief, error, heresy, and tradition that came in through religion to come out in the name of Jesus.

- I command all spirits from my past that are hindering my present and future to come out in the name of Jesus.

- I command all ancestral spirits that entered through my ancestors to come out in the name of Jesus.

> I command all hidden spirits hiding in any part of my life to come out in the name of Jesus.

Day Twenty five *Fri Sept 2, 2016*

Before you pray please follow the instructions below.

a. **Read the Bible Passage below**

   Psalm 91:7

b. **Confess all your sins, both known and unknown**

30 PRAYER POINTS for Protection and destruction of enemies 1

- I cancel my name, my family and Ministry from the death register, with the fire of God, in the name of Jesus.
- Every weapon of destruction fashioned against me, be destroyed by the fire of God, in the name of Jesus.

- Fire of God, fight for me in every area of my life, in Jesus' name.
- Every hindrance to my protection, be melted by the fire of God, in the name of Jesus.
- Every evil gathering against me, be scattered by the thunder fire of God, in the name of Jesus.
- O Lord, let Your fire destroy every evil list containing my name, in the name of Jesus.
- All failures of the past, be converted to success and miracles, in Jesus' name.
- O Lord, let the former rain, the latter rain and Your blessing pour down on me now.
- O Lord, let all the failure mechanism of the enemy designed against my success, be frustrated, in the name of Jesus.
- I receive power from on high and I paralyze all the powers of darkness that are diverting my blessings, in the name of Jesus.
- Beginning from this day, I employ the services of the angels of God to open unto me every door of opportunity and breakthroughs, in the name of Jesus.
- I will not go round in circles again, I will make progress, in the name of Jesus.

- I shall not build for another to inhabit and I shall not plant for another to eat, in the name of Jesus.
- I paralyze the powers of the emptier concerning my Ministry, in the name of Jesus.
- O Lord, let every locust, caterpillar and palm-worm assigned to eat the fruit of my labour be roasted by the fire of God.
- The enemy shall not spoil my testimony in the name of Jesus.
- I reject every backward journey in my life, in the name of Jesus.
- I paralyze every strongman attached to any area of my life, in the name of Jesus.
- Let every agent of shame fashioned to work against my life be paralyzed, in the name of Jesus.
- I paralyze the activities of household wickedness over my life, in the name of Jesus.
- I quench every strange fire emanating from evil tongues against me, in the name of Jesus.
- Lord, give me power for maximum achievement at all round. in Jesus name

- O Lord, give me comforting authority to achieve my goal.
- Lord, fortify me with Your power.
- I paralyze every spirit of disobedience in my life, in Jesus' name.
- I refuse to disobey the voice of God, in the name of Jesus.
- Every root of rebellion in my life, be uprooted, in Jesus' name.
- Fountain of rebellion in my life, dry up, in the name of Jesus.
- Contrary powers fueling rebellion in my life, die, in Jesus' name.
- Every inspiration of witchcraft in my family, be destroyed, in the name of Jesus.

Day Twenty Six *Sat Sept 3, 2016*

Before you pray please follow the instructions below.

a. **Read the Bible Passage below**

   2 Corinthians 4:8-9

b. **Confess all your sins, both known and unknown**

30 PRAYER POINTS for Protection and destruction of Enemies 2

> 31. Blood of Jesus, blot out every evil mark of witchcraft in my life, in the name of Jesus.

> 32. Every garment put upon me by witchcraft, be torn to pieces, in the name of Jesus.

> 33. Angels of God, begin to pursue my household enemies, let their ways be dark and slippery, in the name of Jesus.

> 34. Lord, confuse them and turn them against themselves.

> 35. I break every evil unconscious agreement with household enemies concerning my miracles, in the name of Jesus.

- 36. Household witchcraft, fall down and die, in the name of Jesus.
- 37. O Lord, drag all the household wickedness to the dead sea and bury them there.
- 38. O Lord, I refuse to follow the evil pattern of my household enemies. *in The Name of Jesus*
- 39. My life, jump out from the cage of household wickedness, in the name of Jesus.
- 40. I command all my blessings and potentials buried by wicked household enemies to be exhumed, in the name of Jesus.
- 41. I will see the goodness of the Lord in the land of the living, in the name of Jesus.
- 42. Everything done against me to spoil my joy, receive destruction, in the name of Jesus.
- 43. O Lord, as Abraham received favor in Your eyes, let me receive Your favor, so that I can excel in every area of my life. *in The Name of Jesus*
- 44. Lord Jesus, deal bountifully with me in this month
- 45. It does not matter, whether I deserve it or not, I receive immeasurable favor from the Lord, in the name of Jesus.
- 46. Every blessing God has attributed to me in this year will not pass me by, in the name of Jesus.

47. My blessing will not be transferred to my neighbor in this year, in the name of Jesus.

48. Father Lord, disgrace every power that is out to thwart Your programme for my life, in the name of Jesus.

49. Every step I take shall lead to outstanding success, in Jesus' name.

50. I shall prevail with man and with God in every area of my life, in the name of Jesus.

51. Every habitation of infirmity in my life, break to pieces, in the name of Jesus.

52. My body, soul and spirit, reject every evil load, in Jesus' name.

53. Evil foundation in my life, I pull you down today, in the mighty name of Jesus.

54. Every inherited sickness in my life, depart from me now, in the name of Jesus.

55. Every evil water in my body, get out, in the name of Jesus.

56. I cancel the effect of every evil dedication in my life, in the name of Jesus.

57. Holy Ghost fire, immunize my blood against satanic poisoning, in the name of Jesus.

- 58. Father Lord, put self control in my mouth, in the name of Jesus.

- 59. I refuse to get used to ill health, in the name of Jesus.

- 60. Every door open to infirmity in my life, be permanently closed today, in the name of Jesus.

- 61. Every power contenting with God in my life, be roasted, in the name of Jesus.

- 62. Every power preventing God's glory from manifesting in my life, be paralyzed, in the name of Jesus.

- 63. I loose myself from the spirit of desolation, in the name of Jesus.

- 64. Let God be God in my home, in the name of Jesus.

- 65. Let God be God in my health, in the name of Jesus.

- 66. Let God be God in my career, in the name of Jesus.

- 67. Let God be God in my economy, in the name of Jesus.

- 68. Glory of God, envelope every department of my life, in the name of Jesus.

- 69. The Lord that answereth by fire, be my God, in the name of Jesus.

Day Twenty Seven *Sun Sept 4, 2016*

Before you pray please follow the instructions below.

   a. **Read the Bible Passage below**

   Nahum 1:7
   b. **Confess all your sins, both known and unknown**

30 PRAYER POINTS for Protection and destruction of enemies 3

- Blood of Jesus, cry against all evil gatherings arranged for my sake, in the name of Jesus.
- Father Lord, convert all my past failures to unlimited victories, in the name of Jesus.
- Lord Jesus, create room for my advancement in every area of my life.
- All evil thoughts against me, Lord turn them to be good for me.
- Father Lord, give evil men for my life where evil decisions have been taken against me, in the name of Jesus.
  - Lord, advertise Your dumbfounding prosperity in my life.
- Let the showers of dumbfounding prosperity fall in every department of my life, in the name of Jesus.
- I claim all my prosperity in this week, in the name of Jesus.
- Every door of my prosperity that has been shut, be opened now, in the name of Jesus.
  - Lord, convert my poverty to prosperity, in the name of Jesus.
  - Lord, convert my mistake to perfection, in the name of Jesus.

- Lord, convert my frustration to fulfillment, in the name of Jesus.
- Lord, bring honey out of the rock for me, in the name of Jesus.

> I stand against every evil covenant of sudden death, in the name of Jesus.

> I break every conscious and unconscious evil covenant of untimely death, in the name of Jesus.

> You spirit of death and hell, you have no document in my life, in the name of Jesus.

> You stones of death, depart from my ways, in the name of Jesus.

- Lord, make me a voice of deliverance and blessing. in The Name of Jesus.

> I tread upon the high places of the enemies, in the name of Jesus.

> I bind and render useless, every blood sucking demon, in the name of Jesus.

> You evil current of death, loose your grip over my life, in the name of Jesus.

> I frustrate the decisions of the evil openers in my family, in the name of Jesus.

> Fire of protection, cover my family, in the name of Jesus.

- Lord, make my way perfect, in the name of Jesus.
- Throughout the days of my life, I shall not be put to shame, in the name of Jesus.
- I reject every garment of shame, in the name of Jesus.
- I reject every shoe of shame, in the name of Jesus.
- I reject every head-gear and cap of shame, in the name of Jesus.
- Shamefulness shall not be my lot, in the name of Jesus.
- Every demonic limitation of my progress as a result of shame, be removed, in the name of Jesus.

Day Twenty Eight   Mon Sept 5, 2016

Before you pray please follow the instructions below.

a. **Read the Bible Passage below**

   Psalm 34:19

b. **Confess all your sins, both known and unknown**

30 PRAYER POINTS for Protection and destruction of enemies 4

- Every network of shame around me, be paralyzed, in the name of Jesus.
- Those who seek for my shame shall die for my sake, in the name of Jesus.
- As far as shame is concerned, I shall not record any point for satan, in the name of Jesus.
- In the name of Jesus, I shall not eat the bread of sorrow, I shall not eat the bread of shame and I shall not eat the bread of defeat.
- No evil will touch me throughout my life, in the name of Jesus.

- In this year, I shall reach my goal, in the name of Jesus.
- In every area of my life, my enemies will not catch me, in the name of Jesus.
- In every area of my life, I shall run and not grow weary, I shall walk and shall not faint.
- Lord, in every area of my life, let not my life disgrace You.
- I will not be a victim of failure and I shall not bite my finger for any reason, in the name of Jesus.
- Help me O Lord, to meet up with God's standard for my life. *in the Name of Jesus.*
- I refuse to be a candidate to the spirit of amputation, in the name of Jesus.
- With each day of my life, I shall move to higher ground, in the name of Jesus.
- Every spirit of shame set in motion against my life, I bind you, in the name of Jesus.
- Every spirit competing with my breakthroughs, be chained, in the name of Jesus.
- I bind every spirit of slavery, in the name of Jesus.
- In every day of my life, I disgrace all my stubborn pursuers, in the name of Jesus.

- I bind, every spirit of Herod, in the name of Jesus.
- Every spirit challenging my God, be disgraced, in Jesus' name.
- Every Red Sea before me, be parted, in the name of Jesus.
- I command every spirit of bad ending to be bound in every area of my life, in the name of Jesus.
- Every spirit of Saul, be disgraced in my life, in the name of Jesus.
- Every spirit of Pharaoh, be disgraced in my life, in Jesus' name.
- I reject every evil invitation to backwardness, in Jesus' name.
- I command every stone of hindrance in my life to be rolled away, in the name of Jesus.
- Father Lord, roll away every stone of poverty from my life, in the name Jesus.
- Let every stone of infertility in my marriage be rolled away, in the name of Jesus.
- Let every stone of non-achievement in my life be rolled away, in the name of Jesus.
- My God, roll away every stone of hardship and slavery from my life, in the name of Jesus.

> My God, roll away every stone of failure planted in my life, my home and in my Ministries, in the name of Jesus. *(Business, Finances)*

> You stones of hindrance, planted at the edge of my breakthroughs, be rolled away, in the name of Jesus.

Day Twenty Nine *Tues Spt 6, 2016*

Before you pray please follow the instructions below.

   a. **Read the Bible Passage below**

   Psalm 121:3

   b. **Confess all your sins, both known and unknown**

30 PRAYER POINTS for Protection and destruction of enemies 5

- **You stones of stagnancy, stationed at the border of my life, be rolled away, in the name of Jesus.**

- My God, let every storm of the 'amputator' planted at the beginning of my life, at the middle of my life and at the end of my life, be rolled away, in the name of Jesus.

- Father Lord, I thank You for all the stones You have rolled away, I forbid their return, in the name of Jesus.

- Let the power from above come upon me, in the name of Jesus.

- Father Lord, advertize Your power in every area of my life, in the name of Jesus.

- Father Lord, make me a power generator, throughout the days of my life, in the name of Jesus.

- Let the power to live a holy life throughout the days of my life fall upon me, in the name of Jesus.

- Let the power to live a victorious life throughout the days of my life fall upon me, in the name of Jesus.

- Let the power to prosper throughout the days of my life fall upon me, in the name of Jesus.

- Let the power to be in good health throughout the days of my life fall upon me, in the name of Jesus.

- Let the power to disgrace my enemies throughout the days of my life fall upon me, in the name of Jesus.
- Let the power of Christ rest upon me now, in the name of Jesus.
- Let the power to bind and loose fall upon me now, in the name of Jesus.
- Father Lord, let Your key of revival unlock every department of my life for Your revival fire, in the name of Jesus.
- Every area of my life that is at the point of death, receive the touch of revival, in the name of Jesus.
- Father Lord, send down Your fire and anointing into my life, in the name of Jesus.
- Every uncrucified area in my life, receive the touch of fire and be crucified, in the name of Jesus.
- Let the fire fall and consume all hindrances to my advancement, in the name of Jesus.
- You stubborn problems in my life, receive the Holy Ghost dynamite, in the name of Jesus.
- You carry-over miracle from my past fasting and prayer programmes, receive the touch of fire and be materialized, in the name of Jesus.
- Holy Ghost fire, baptize me with prayer miracle, in Jesus' name.

- Every area of my life that needs deliverance, receive the touch of fire and be delivered, in the name of Jesus.

- Let my angels of blessing locate me now, in the name of Jesus.

- Every satanic programme of impossibility, I cancel you now, in the name of Jesus.

- Every household wickedness and its programme of impossibility, be paralyzed, in the name of Jesus.

- No curse will land on my head or my Ministry, in the name of Jesus.

- Throughout the days of my life, I will not waste money on my health: the Lord shall be my healer, in the name of Jesus.

- Throughout the days of my life, I will be in the right place at the right time.

- Throughout the days of my life, I will not depart from the fire of God's protection, in the name of Jesus.

Day Thirty Wed Sept 7, 2016

Lord before I finish This prayer, I need AN uncommon outstanding miracle in Every area of my life in The Name of Jesus.

Before you pray please follow the instructions below.

a. **Read the Bible Passage below**

   Isaiah 50:7

b. **Confess all your sins, both known and unknown**

30 PRAYER POINTS for Protection and destruction of enemies 6

- Throughout the days of my life, I will not be a candidate for incurable disease, in the name of Jesus.
- Every weapon of captivity, be disgraced by fire, in the name of Jesus.
- Lord, before I finish this prayer, I need an outstanding miracle in every area of my life. *in The Name of Jesus*
- Let every attack planned against the progress of my life be frustrated, in the name of Jesus.
- I command the spirits of harassment and torment to leave me, in the name of Jesus.
- Lord, begin to speak soundness into my mind and being. *Now in The Name of Jesus*

✶✶ ➤ **I reverse every witchcraft curse issued against my progress, in the name of Jesus.**

➤ **I condemn all the spirits condemning me, in the name of Jesus.**

➤ Let divine accuracy come into my life and operations, in the name of Jesus.

➤ No evil directive will manifest in my life, in the name of Jesus.

✶ ➤ **Let the plans and purposes of heaven be fulfilled in my life and ministry, in the name of Jesus.**

Genuine/compatible →
- Lord, bring to me friends that reverence Your name and keep all others away. *in The Name of Jesus*

✶ ➤ **Let divine strength come into my life, in the name of Jesus.**

- Lord, cause Yourself to be real in my life. *Right Now in The Name of Jesus*
- Lord, show Yourself in my life today.

✶ ➤ **Let every stronghold working against my peace be destroyed, in the name of Jesus.**

→ ➤ **Let the power to destroy every decree of darkness operating in my life fall upon me now, in the name of Jesus.**

➤ Lord, deliver my tongue from evil silence. *in The Name of Jesus.*

- Lord, let my tongue tell others of Your life.
- Lord, loose my tongue and use it for Your glory.
- Lord, let my tongue bring straying sheep back to the fold.
- Lord, let my tongue strengthen those who are discouraged. *in The Name of Jesus*
- Lord, let my tongue guide the sad and the lonely.
- Lord, baptize my tongue with love and fire. *in The Name of Jesus*
- Let every unrepentant and stubborn pursuers be disgraced in my life, in the name of Jesus.
- Let every iron-like curse working against my life be broken by the blood of Jesus, in the name of Jesus.
- Let every problem designed to disgrace me receive open shame, in the name of Jesus.
- Let every problem anchor in my life be uprooted, in Jesus' name.
- Multiple evil covenants, be broken by the blood of Jesus, in the name of Jesus.
- Multiple curses, be broken by the blood of Jesus, in Jesus' name.

Day Thirty One *Thurs Sept 8, 2016*

Before you pray please follow the instructions below.

   a. **Read the Bible Passage below**

   John 10:28-30

   b. **Confess all your sins, both known and unknown**

18 PRAYER POINTS for Protection and destruction of enemies 7

- Every day The Kingdom of God + The Kingdom of Heaven Manifests in me
- Everyday God use me as a mighty arrow in His Hand to Bless someone with Words of Encouragement

- Everything done against me with evil padlocks, be nullified by the blood of Jesus, in the name of Jesus.

- Everything done against me at any cross-roads, be nullified by the blood of Jesus, in the name of Jesus.

- Let every stubborn and prayer resisting demon receive stones of fire and thunder, in the name of Jesus.

- Every stubborn and prayer resisting sickness, loose your evil hold upon my life, in the name of Jesus.

- Every problem associated with the dead, be smashed by the blood of Jesus, in the name of Jesus.

- I recover *All* my stolen property seven fold, in the name of Jesus.

- Let every evil memory about me be erased by the blood of Jesus, in the name of Jesus.

- I disallow my breakthroughs from being caged, by forces of darkness in Jesus' name.

- Let the sun of my prosperity arise and scatter every cloud of poverty, in the name of Jesus.

- I decree unstoppable advancement upon my life and ministry, in Jesus' name.

- I soak every day of my life in the blood of Jesus and in *miracle* signs and wonders, in the name of Jesus.

Know This → I decree That Everyday I soak, saturate and marinate my life in The Blood of Jesus and in signs, wonders & mighty miracles in The Name of Jesus

I break every stronghold of financial debt in my life in the name of Jesus

- *I soak, saturate & marinate my finances/debts in the blood of Jesus in the name of Jesus / finances/debts*

- I break every stronghold of oppression in my life and marriage, in Jesus' name.
- Let every satanic joy about my life be terminated, in the name of Jesus.
- I paralyze every household wickedness, in the name of Jesus.
- Let every satanic spreading river dry up by the blood of Jesus, in the name of Jesus.
- I bind every ancestral spirit and command them to loose their hold over my life, in the name of Jesus.
- Ancestral spirits, pack your loads and go out of my life, in the name of Jesus.
- Every curse of profitless work in my life break by the fire of Holy Ghost. *in the name of Jesus*

I decree that all my caged & padlocked finances are being released right now in the name of Jesus. ~ by the fire of God

Day Thirty Two *Fri Sept 9, 2016*

Before you pray please follow the instructions below.

a. Read the following Bible Passages

Philippians 4:19, Jeremiah 29:11

b. **Confess all your sins, both known and unknown**

49 PRAYER POINTS for Release of Blessings

- Thank God for His goodness, mercy, love and provisions.
- Confess and repent of all sins, known and unknown.
- Touch your lips and confess this: "my mouth is anointed with the power of God Almighty".
- I decree that every word that come out of my mouth as I pray today must be fulfilled in Jesus' name.
- Lord, open doors of opportunity to me through this prayer, in the name of Jesus.
- I receive the anointing of restoration in Jesus' name.
- Every person or personality who has taken what belongs to me; I command them to release it in Jesus' name.
- Powers denying me my due miracles, receive the stones of fire, in the name of Jesus.

- I bind and cast out every strong man in my life, family or environment who refuses to release my blessings, breakthrough, miracle, promotion or prosperity in Jesus' name.
- I bind the spirit of depression, frustration and disillusionment in my life, in the name of Jesus.
- I command all evil unknown forces organised against my life to be scattered, in the name of Jesus.
- I paralyze every activity of physical and spiritual parasites and devourers in my life, in the name of Jesus.
- I retrieve back from the hands of the enemy any of my possession that I unknowingly misplaced, in Jesus' name.
- I recover all the ground that I had lost to the enemy, in Jesus' name
- I command all the damages done to my life by . . . (pick from the under listed) to be repaired, in the name of Jesus. *(GREED, OVEREATING)*
- I command seven-fold restoration of everything the enemy has taken from me, in Jesus' name.
- Fire of God, consume the evil clock of the enemy that is working against my life, in the name of Jesus.
- Oh LORD, restore my wasted years in Jesus' name.

- LORD, restore my wasted efforts, money, health, strength and blessings, in Jesus' name.
- I remove from my life by fire every barrier to my breakthroughs in Jesus' name.
- I uproot and destroy from my life by the Holy Ghost fire every obstacle to my miracle, in Jesus' name.
- I break in pieces every horn scattering my blessings, in the name of Jesus Christ.
- I destroy every hedge the enemy has put over my blessings to prevent me from receiving them in my lifetime, in Jesus' name.
- Every evil power holding back my prayers, or the answers to my prayer, I command you to be bound, in Jesus' name.
- . I command all doors of good things, closed against me by the enemy to be opened, in the name of Jesus.
- I release my helper to come to me now, in Jesus' name.
- Every shadow of darkness the enemy has cast over me, to prevent my prosperity, job, business contacts, promotion, or breakthrough from locating me, I remove it by fire, in the name of Jesus Christ.

- Let all hidden potentials and gifts that will make me great, stolen from me, be restored 21 fold, in the name of Jesus.

- I decree total destruction upon every personality that has vowed never to release to me anything God has destined for me, in Jesus' name.

- I break in pieces every covenant or curse obstructing divine restoration in my life, in Jesus' name.

- Trees of problems in my life, dry up to the roots, in Jesus' name.

- Walls of physical and spiritual opposition, fall after the order of Jericho, in the name of Jesus

- Lord, make my case a miracle. Shock my foes, friends, and even myself, in the name of Jesus.

- With the blood of Jesus Christ, I shatter every covenant that gives the enemy upper hand to take from me the blessings God has given to me, in the name of Jesus Christ.

- Every household wickedness eating up the blessings God Almighty has bestowed upon my life and family, I destroy you, in Jesus' name.

- Let my king Uzziah die, so that I can see Your face, O Lord, in the name of Jesus.

- I command a hundred-fold restoration of everything the enemy took from me when I was weak, in Jesus' name.

- I destroy by fire all the horns assigned to scatter my prosperity, family, business and possessions, in Jesus' name.

- I demolish every stumbling block on my way to success, promotion and victory, in Jesus' name.

- Every good thing God has destined for me, but is in the possession of someone else, I command it to come to me now, in Jesus' name.

- I posses the power to pursue, overtake and recover my goods from spiritual Egyptians, in the name of Jesus.

- Let every spell, jinxes, and demonic incantations rendered against me be cancelled, in the name of Jesus.

- Lord, heal all wounds and spiritual bullets sustained from attacks of the enemy.

- Father, I pray, remove any person or personality sitting on my blessings, miracles, breakthrough, prosperity, finance, job or good health, in the name of Jesus Christ.

- All my possessions in the north, south, east or west, I command them to come to me now, in Jesus' name.

- All my possessions in the spirit realm, I release them into the physical by fire, in the name of Jesus Christ.
- I receive a hundred-fold restoration of all I have lost, in Jesus' name.
- I receive a hundred-fold restoration of everything the enemy stole from me, in the name of Jesus Christ.
- Lord, give me power for a new beginning.
- Thank God for answers to your prayers.

IF YOU ENJOY THIS BOOK RATE IT OR IF YOU HAVE A TESTIMONY AS A RESULT OF YOUR READING THIS BOOK PLEASE SHARE IT OR YOU CAN ALSO RATE IT. YOU MAY ALSO SEND ALL TESTIMONIES TO

info@olusolacoker.com

Other Books

Click on the Image below to read other books by the Author

Repeat Day 2
Day 9 – Finances
Day 11 – Promotion
Day 17 – Excellence 6 (yr of unusual greatness / Isaiah 45:1-3)
Treasure of darkness
Day 19 – uncommon Breakthrough
Day 22 – uncommon Breakthrough

Guaranteed Powerful Prayers for Financial and Business Breakthroughs

350 Life Changing Prayers for Daily Breakthroughs

By
Dr Olusola Coker

① Start – Aug 10, 2016 – End (Day 1)
Sept 10, 2016 – D32

HARNESSING YOUR DESTINY

Dr Olusola Coker

Day 12 Sat Aug 20, 2016 – Found Pink Feather on porch on Hornadi

Day 13 Sun Aug 21, 2016 –
* I preached at Shiloh for Pastor Dowell
* Floyd + Vera Daniels from Miami FL were at my house to possibly buy it. Her father lives in Bucanan, VA + having open heart surgery on Tues. (SAW Rainbow on 68 coming to Greensboro Today)

5613-

Made in the USA
Lexington, KY
01 August 2016